© Claire Crean, 2024
All rights reserved. No part of this book may be reproduced or utilized in any form or by any means, electronic or mechanical, including photocopying, recording, or by any information storage and retrieval system, without permission in writing from the author.

To my mother, who always inspired me to unleash my creativity and dream big.

Jazzcat: The Cool Cat Who Followed His Musical Dreams! is a delightful children's book that tells the story of a stylish and curious cat named Jazzcat. He's immediately captivated when Jazzcat stumbles upon a golden saxophone at a yard sale. With determination and a love for jazz, Jazzcat learns to play the saxophone, becoming a musical sensation in his neighborhood. Every week, pets gather to hear his smooth jazz tunes, which bring joy and inspiration to all who listen. Jazzcat's story is a charming tale of following your passions, staying humble, and spreading happiness through music. Perfect for young readers, this book encourages children to dream big and pursue what they love. Join Jazzcat on his journey and discover how a little music can make a big difference!

♩azzcat

The Cool Cat Who Followed His Musical Dreams!

Written by Claire Crean

Illustrated by Kiran Akram

Jazzcat, the coolest cat in town, was out for a stroll when he stumbled upon a yard sale. The people thought he was just too cute to resist, so they let him explore all the cool things!

As Jazzcat checked out the treasures, something shiny caught his eye—a golden, gleaming saxophone next to a tree. It made him freeze right in his tracks!

A golden saxophone was just waiting for him. The tag said "$10." He dropped his ten-dollar bill and dashed home with his new treasure.

At home, Jazzcat watched videos and learned how to play. He practiced and practiced until he became a saxophone pro!

Every week, the neighborhood pets gather
in the park to hear Jazzcat
play his tunes.

Jazzcat plays any song the animals request. They wag their tails, tap their paws, and sing along. Paws go tap, tap, tap, and clap, clap, clap!

Jazzcat's owners have no idea about his secret talent. To them, the saxophone is just a toy. They know he loves jazz and fancy suits, but they don't know he's really a musician.

Every day, Jazzcat follows his dream by playing music that makes everyone happy. Smooth jazz calms and inspires his friends, just like it did for him.

What about you? What's your dream?
Jazzcat followed his and guess what?
You can follow yours, too!

THE END

About The Author

Claire Crean's passion for reading and writing began at a young age. She earned an English degree at Florida State University and has spent years immersing herself in literature. Claire's creativity and love for storytelling have culminated in her debut children's book, Jazzcat. She is thrilled to bring her childhood character to life and hopes to inspire young readers to dream big and embrace their creativity!

Made in the USA
Middletown, DE
26 March 2025